About this book

... in 60 seconds

You might think there are a lot of human beings in the world – but the number of people is nothing compared to the number of insects. For every human being on the planet, there are millions and millions and MILLIONS of insects! And even though they are much smaller than us, they take up more space and weigh more than all the humans on Earth put together.

That's partly because while there's only one species, or type, of human, there are almost a million different species of insects (there are 400,000 types of beetles alone)! And every year, scientists discover and name hundreds of new ones.

So it's no surprise that we often bump into insects – a fly buzzing around your kitchen, a butterfly fluttering around your garden or park, or a cockroach hiding in a food cupboard. We share our lives with insects, and they love sharing our food, flowers and leftovers with us. In fact, insects live almost everywhere in the world, in almost every type of habitat. Beaches, fields, soil, underground caves, high mountains, tropical jungles, scorching deserts, rivers and lakes all have insects living in them. There are even insects that survive in the freezing cold of Antarctica.

Insects are incredibly important to humans, and they affect our lives in all kinds of ways. True, some of the ways are bad, like spreading deadly diseases in their bites, or munching on our crops and food stores (or even on our favourite clothes!). But insects also bring us many benefits – from supplying us with honey, beeswax or silk, to spreading pollen between plants, so that fruits and seeds can form to feed us. In fact, without insects, our lives would be very different...

In this book every topic has a page to read as fast as you like to grasp the main facts quickly, a full-page colour picture, and a handy sum-up. Try the missions you'll find throughout – and discover even more about these awesome tiny animals.

8

Insect bodies

If someone asked you to draw a quick picture of an insect, you'd probably sketch something with a body, a head, six legs and two antennae or feelers. And if you did, you'd be spot on! Although insects come in a huge variety of shapes and sizes, they all have this same, basic body plan – sometimes with one or two pairs of wings as well. There's another thing insects have in common, too – they are all on the small side, with none growing much bigger than a page in this book.

Insect bodies
Glossary

abdomen The back section of an insect's body and often the largest part. It holds the most important organs, such as the heart.

antenna (plural antennae) One of two sensitive feelers on top of an insect's head.

arthropod (ar-thro-pod) The scientific name for an animal that has an exoskeleton, a body divided into sections, and jointed legs. Insects, spiders and crabs are all arthropods.

chitin The hard material that an insect's exoskeleton is made from. It can be thick and stiff like a shell, or thin and flexible.

compound eye An eye divided into many smaller eyes. Each mini-eye sees a single image and the insect's brain forms all the images into one big picture.

elytra (el-i-tra, singular elytron) Hard wing-cases that cover and protect a ladybird or other beetle's delicate flying wings and abdomen.

exoskeleton The stiff, strong outer skeleton that protects an insect's soft body and gives it shape.

head The front section of an insect where the antennae, eyes and mouthparts are located.

larva (plural larvae) A worm-like baby insect that looks different from its parents.

ocellus (o-sell-us, plural ocelli) A simple insect eye that can only see light and dark.

ommatidium (omma-ti-dium, plural ommatidia) The scientific name for the single 'mini-eye' piece of a compound eye.

spiracles Tiny breathing holes in an insect's exoskeleton that let in air, so that oxygen reaches the insect's organs and keeps it alive.

thorax The middle section of an insect's body, where the legs and wings are attached.

Body plan
... in 30 seconds

One of the best ways to identify an insect is to count its legs. An adult insect has six legs, two antennae or feelers, and three main body sections. Baby insects, or larvae, can look quite different from their parents.

Counting legs helps you tell insects apart from spiders, scorpions, mites and ticks – all which have eight legs – or centipedes and millipedes, which have many more.

Insects use the two antennae on their head for sensing smells in the air. Sometimes they use them to touch and feel other insects. Ants often touch each other with their antennae to pass on messages. Antennae shapes range from long and thin to short and stubby, spoon-shaped, fringed or feather-shaped.

An insect's three body sections are the head, thorax or middle section, and abdomen. The eyes, mouth and antennae are on the head. The three pairs of legs are attached to the thorax, as well as the wings if the insect has them (not all insects do). The abdomen is often the largest part and contains most of the organs, such as the stomach and intestines.

3-second sum-up

Insects have six legs, three body sections and two antennae.

3-minute mission Which is which?

Do you know which of these creatures are insects, and which aren't? Use the Internet to help you.

Mosquito • Head louse • Tarantula • Firefly • Snail • Dust mite • Flea • Moth • Scorpion • Woodlouse

Answers on page 96

Jointed legs

... in 30 seconds

Insects belong to a group of animals called arthropods. The name 'arthropod' means 'jointed legs', and spiders, centipedes, crabs and lobsters are arthropods, too.

The joints in an insect's legs allow the legs to bend and move, just as the joints in our own limbs do. Insect legs are different from ours, though, because they don't have bones inside them, only muscles. The legs are made of chitin instead, a tough material that is a bit like fingernails.

A typical insect leg is made up of sections connected by joints. Muscles inside the sections pull the leg into different positions, so that the insect can walk, run or jump. The champion insect runner, the Australian tiger beetle, can zoom along at up to 9 km (5.6 miles) per hour. This beetle is only 2 cm (0.8 inches) long, so it's covering 125 times its own body length every second. A human doing the same thing would be running as fast as a flying jumbo jet!

Insects can sometimes lose a leg or two in a fight with a hungry predator, such as a bird or lizard. Some insects, such as cockroaches and praying mantises, can regrow all or part of a missing leg.

3-second sum-up

Insects have jointed legs to help them move around.

3-minute mission Leg survey!

Next time you find a fly, moth or earwig in your house, catch it under a glass (ask an adult to help) and look at it closely. Can you see how many joints each leg has, and how they move? Remember to let it go once you've had a good look.

Although all insects have jointed legs, the legs don't all look the same. Some are specially shaped for making particular moves.

Backswimmers have extra-large back legs that they use like oars while swimming.

Grasshoppers have very big back legs, with powerful jumping muscles inside.

A praying mantis has big front legs armed with spikes for grabbing its prey.

Tiger beetles, which are good at running fast, have long, skinny legs.

Exoskeletons

... in 30 seconds

Inside your body is a framework of hard, rigid bones holding you up – your skeleton. But insects have no skeleton inside them. How do they stay up?

An insect's skeleton – called an exoskeleton – is on the outside. It's a strong, protective covering, made mainly of tough, flexible chitin. A bit like plastic, chitin can be thick and rigid, like a beetle's hard shell, or thinner and bendy. This means that some parts of the exoskeleton can be softer and more flexible than other parts, so that the insect can wriggle and move around.

The exoskeleton holds the insect's body together and gives it shape, protects it from enemy attack and also stops it from drying out. Tiny holes called spiracles let in air, so that the insect can take in oxygen.

Exoskeletons have many colours and patterns. Bright colours can warn predators that the insect is poisonous, and dull colours can help it blend in with its surroundings. As some insect young grow bigger, they shed their exoskeletons until they finally become adults. The new soft covering beneath hardens and dries to form a new, bigger exoskeleton.

3-second sum-up

An insect's exoskeleton is a tough covering that gives it strength and protection.

3-minute mission Pebble beetles

You need: • Oval, beetle-shaped pebbles • Old nail varnish, marker pens or paints

Turn pale-coloured pebbles into beetles by painting or colouring them with spots, stripes or other patterns. Can you make a camouflaged beetle that could hide in the grass or on a tree trunk?

Insects have a strong skeleton on the outside of their body.

These male stag beetles are fighting.

Organs and muscles are packed inside the tough exoskeleton.

The nervous system.

The heart and blood vessels.

The hard exoskeleton is like armour.

Breathing tubes carrying oxygen.

The legs are made of the same hardened material.

The crop, or food tube.

Milkweed beetles store bitter-tasting chemicals in their bodies. Their bright red markings warn predators away.

This cricket has shed its old exoskeleton, which looks like a papery ghost.

Insect wings

... in 30 seconds

An insect's wings grow out of its exoskeleton and are made of the same material, chitin. Muscles attached to the exoskeleton make the wings flap, so the insect can fly.

Insect wings are so thin they are often see-through, but they have a network of veins that strengthens them. Butterfly and moth wings are also covered in tiny scales, giving them bright patterns.

Most insects, including bees, wasps, mayflies, dragonflies and beetles, have two pairs of wings – four in all. The wings have to be in pairs to give the insect balance – otherwise it would fly in circles! A beetle's front pair of wings are hardened into stiff wing-cases called elytra. The beetle usually keeps its flying wings folded up underneath its elytra.

Some types of insects grow wings when they need them. For example, aphids grow them when food is scarce, so they can fly away and find a new place to live. Insect larvae and nymphs do not have flight wings and some adult insects also have no wings at all. Fleas are brilliant at jumping, so they don't need to fly. Wetas – big, heavy, grasshopper-like insects from New Zealand – hop instead of flying, while wingless silverfish run fast and hide in dark corners.

3-second sum-up

Most insects have four wings, some only have two and some don't have any.

Bzzzzzzz!

How fast can you flap your arms? The buzzing noise insects make is the sound of their wings flapping many times every second. Houseflies and honeybees can beat their wings over 200 times a second, but some insects are even faster. One species of midge, a type of small biting fly, can beat its wings 1,040 times a second!

Flying insects have either two or four wings, which grow in pairs from the exoskeleton.

It takes off into the air.

It lifts the elytra (wing-cases) so the flying wings can spring open.

Once the flying wings are fully extended, the ladybird can start flapping.

The ladybird gets ready to take off.

A ladybird, which is a type of beetle, prepares to fly by lifting its elytra and opening out its folded wings.

Insect eyes

... in 30 seconds

Insects have eyes that work in a very different way to ours. In fact, they have two types of eyes, and each insect has one type, the other type, or both.

The big, bulging eyes you see on a fly are called compound eyes. They are actually made up of many smaller eyes joined together. Each mini-eye, called an ommatidium, sees its own image of the world. The insect's brain pieces together all these mini-images – they are a bit like pixels on a computer screen – to build up a big picture of everything around it.

The other type of insect eyes are called ocelli. They are small, simple eyes that can't see very clearly, but are good at detecting light and dark.

Some insects, like earwigs for example, only have compound eyes. Other insects, like fleas, only have ocelli – usually a few of them on each side of the head. And some insects, like wasps and ants, have two large compound eyes and a number of ocelli as well.

Not all insects see colours. But some, like butterflies, have brilliant colour vision to help them find flowers.

3-second sum-up

Most insects have big compound eyes, simple ocelli, or a mixture of both!

3-minute mission See like a fly!

You need: • Pencil • Bubble wrap • Card • Scissors • Sticky tape

1 Draw a pair of glasses on the card. You could trace around a real pair.

2 Cut out your glasses. Ask an adult to cut out holes for the lenses.

3 Cut out pieces of bubble wrap for the lenses, and tape them in place.

4 Now put on your fly eyes and see the world through compound eyes!

Some insects see the world in lots of mini-images. Other insects can only see light and dark.

Fleas have two simple ocellus eyes. They can only see light and dark.

Dragonflies have large compound eyes and use their sharp eyesight for chasing prey.

A compound eye

Large compound eyes are made of lots of mini-eyes. Each one sends a single picture to the insect's brain.

An ocellus

Tiny ocelli have a single lens and simple, light-sensitive cells.

Some insects, such as ants and wasps, have both types of eyes.

Insect life cycles

A life cycle is the series of changes an insect goes through as it is born or hatches from an egg, grows up, finds a mate and then has its own young. In fact, all living things have life cycles. This is to make sure that each type of living thing has babies, so that its species can carry on. Many insects have life cycles with several stages, and can look very different at each stage.

Insect life cycles
Glossary

antenna (plural antennae) One of two sensitive feelers on top of an insect's head.

brood A large group of cicada nymphs, emerging together from their underground burrows.

cell One of the tiny units that make up a living thing. All animals and plants are made of cells.

chrysalis A butterfly pupa.

hatch Break out or emerge from an egg.

instar A stage in an insect's life cycle that is between two periods of moulting.

larva (plural larvae) A worm-like baby insect that looks different from its parents.

life cycle The changes that an animal or plant goes through during its life.

mating The coming together of a male and female insect to reproduce.

metamorphosis (meta-morph-o-sis). The changes, from one form to another, that an insect goes through to become an adult.

moulting When an insect grows too big for its exoskeleton, it bursts out of it. A new, larger exoskeleton underneath replaces the old one.

nocturnal To be active at night and rest during the day.

nymph A baby insect that already looks like an insect, similar to its parents.

pupa The stage in an insect's life cycle when it is changing from a larva into an adult.

sap The fluid that flows inside a tree or plant.

species The scientific name for a type of living thing that can reproduce to make more of the same type, for example, honeybees.

Finding a mate

... in 30 seconds

Like other animals, most insects can only reproduce if a male and a female get together and mate. Cells from the male join together with cells from the female to make eggs that can grow into new insects.

For that to happen, males and females of the same species have to find each other. One way to do this is by smell. Some moths, like the cecropia moth and the giant peacock moth, have such a good sense of smell that a male can locate a female from 2 km (over a mile) away! The males use their very large feathery antennae to pick up the scent.

Morpho butterflies have wings that are camouflaged on the undersides, so when they sit still with their wings up, they are hard to see. But when looking for a mate, they fly around, showing off their bright blue wing tops. Fireflies (a type of beetle) have flashing lights on their bodies to make it even easier to find each other.

Male grasshoppers and cicadas attract females to them with loud chirruping or buzzing noises. A male cicada sits in a tree and vibrates a drum-like part on his abdomen to make a noise of up to 120 decibels – as loud as a chainsaw! Females fly to the loudest males.

3-second sum-up

To mate and have babies, a male and a female from the same species have to meet up.

Ear splitting!

The song of the cicada is the loudest in the insect world. To humans, the sound they make can be almost deafening! If you don't live in a place where they are found, it might be hard to imagine just how loud they are. The next time you hear a screaming siren, or a car horn blasts right next to your ear, or you walk past a noisy road drill, you will get the idea!

Male fireflies attract females by flashing a sequence of lights. Each firefly species makes a different pattern.

This firefly makes a pattern of a quick sequence of flashes, followed by a short flight with no light.

To make this flashing pattern, the firefly swoops in a J-shaped curve each time it flashes its light on.

The female firefly watches the display from a bush or tree, and flashes her own tail to reply to her own species.

The firefly makes light at the tip of its abdomen. It contains a chemical called luciferin that can join with oxygen to make a bright glow.

Hatching out

... in 30 seconds

Like birds, lizards and frogs, most insects reproduce by laying eggs which then hatch out into babies. Insect young come in many different forms.

For example, the eggs of honeybees, houseflies and butterflies hatch into larvae – also called grubs, maggots or caterpillars. These soft, worm-like babies look very different from the adults. A larva must feed and grow, then go through a change called metamorphosis to turn into an adult.

In other insects, like dragonflies and silverfish, the eggs hatch into young called nymphs, which already look quite insect-like. They may be a mini-version of the adult, or look similar. They gradually grow and change into an adult in several stages.

Most insects are pretty small, and their eggs are even smaller! The smallest of all belong to a type of tiny fly. You could line up 50 of its eggs in a single millimetre space on a ruler.

A few insects, such as aphids and tstetse flies, don't lay eggs. Instead, they give birth to live larvae or nymphs.

3-second sum-up

Most (but not all) insects lay eggs, which hatch out into different types of babies.

3-minute mission Egg-spotting

Look for insect eggs like these, especially in spring:

- Ladybird eggs are yellow, long ovals, laid on many types of leaves.
- Painted lady butterfly eggs look like tiny green gooseberries, and are often on thistle or nettle leaves.
- You might see ants' eggs in the soil. They are creamy ovals, often with a spot at one end.

Ladybird eggs laid on the underside of a leaf hatch into small, black ladybird larvae.

Here are several different types of insect eggs that you might find in your house, park or garden – but what will they hatch into?

Painted lady butterfly eggs laid on a leaf hatch into hairy caterpillars.

A silverfish egg laid in the bathroom hatches into a tiny baby silverfish, or nymph.

Housefly eggs laid on rotting fish hatch out into wriggly maggots, a type of larva.

Caterpillars

... in 30 seconds

The life cycle of a butterfly – from egg to caterpillar, to pupa, to adult – is among the best-known of all insect life cycles. But how do those changes really happen?

A typical butterfly, such as a cabbage white, lays eggs on the plant the caterpillars prefer to eat – in this case, a cabbage. About three days later, the eggs hatch and tiny caterpillars, about 4 mm (0.2 inches) long, emerge. They eat their own eggshells, then start munching the cabbage leaves.

Over the next month, the caterpillars grow up to ten times bigger, shedding their skin several times. Once a caterpillar is big enough, it turns into a chrysalis – the name for a butterfly or moth pupa. Its final skin is replaced with a hard, pointed, greenish shell, which hangs by a silk thread from the cabbage plant, a fence or a wall.

Inside the chrysalis, the caterpillar does not simply grow butterfly wings, legs and antennae. Instead, almost all of its body dissolves into a kind of gloopy soup. Then, the ingredients are rearranged, and the body of an adult butterfly gradually forms. This metamorphosis (change) takes about 11 days to complete. Finally, the chrysalis cracks open, and the new butterfly pushes its way out.

3-second sum-up

A butterfly goes through a series of changes to complete its life cycle.

Gleaming gold

Some butterflies, such as the cream-spotted tigerwing from Central America, have a shiny, metallic-looking chrysalis that appears to be made of gold. This is why they were given the name 'chrysalis', which means 'golden'.

The life cycle of the cabbage white butterfly goes from an egg laid by a female adult, to a caterpillar, a chrysalis, and to a new adult.

The female lays her eggs on the underside of a cabbage leaf.

Adult cabbage whites only live for a few weeks. In this time, a male and female meet and mate.

The adult climbs out of the chrysalis.

Like many insects, cabbage white butterflies leave their eggs unattended. The larvae are left to fend for themselves, with no parents to look after them.

Inside, the pupa transforms into an adult.

The fully grown caterpillar transforms into a chrysalis.

Growing up slowly
... in 30 seconds

Unlike humans, many species of insects live for a lot longer as babies than they do as adults. A caterpillar may live for several months, then become a butterfly that lives for a week. A mayfly can spend two years of its life as a nymph, and just a day or two as an adult!

Strangest of all are periodical cicadas, from the forests of North America. There are two types: 13-year cicadas and 17-year cicadas. Depending on the type, the nymphs spend either 13 or 17 years buried under the soil, sucking juices from tree roots.

When their growing period is up, all the cicadas in an area – known as a brood – suddenly emerge from the ground and climb onto trees or bushes, where they turn into flying adults. In a few weeks, they feed on tree sap, find a mate, lay eggs in the trees and die. When they hatch, the newborn nymphs burrow underground – for another 13 or 17 years!

The numbers 13 and 17 are prime numbers. This means that the different types of cicadas very rarely emerge at the same time. So each type of cicada only meets its own type to mate with, and the different types don't have to compete with each other for food.

3-second sum-up

Periodical cicadas, and many other insects, spend a longer time as babies than as adults.

3-minute mission Find the primes

Scientists have noticed that 13 and 17, the numbers of periodical cicadas, are both prime numbers. A prime number is a number that can only be divided by itself and 1.

Write down all the prime numbers you can spot between 1 and 30. Remember that 1 is not counted as a prime number.

How many can you find?

Answers on page 96

Some insects have a very long life cycle. The nymphs of 17-year cicadas spend 17 years underground!

Male cicadas buzz to attract females, and they mate.

Each female lays her eggs in tree twigs.

At first the adults are white, but they darken over a few days.

The nymphs hatch, fall to the ground and burrow down.

They emerge and climb onto trees or bushes, then shed their skin a final time and become adults.

The nymphs go through five stages, or instars, as they feed and grow.

After 17 years, in spring, the whole brood of nymphs burrows towards the surface.

Caring parents

... in 30 seconds

Social insects, such as ants, honeybees and termites, look after their young and feed them as they grow. But the parents – the queen and her mate – don't usually do this job themselves. Instead, it's left to the workers.

Most other insects don't look after their babies. They just lay their eggs in their chosen spot, and leave them there. When the larvae or nymphs hatch out, they have to fend for themselves and find their own food.

But a few insects, such as the common earwig, do care for their own young. After mating in the autumn, a pair of earwigs dig a burrow in the soil. Then the male leaves and the female lays around 50 eggs. During the winter, she stays in her nest, guarding the eggs and making sure they stay at the right temperature, like birds do.

When the nymphs hatch in the spring, the mother keeps them away from predators, such as beetles, and collects food for them. They leave the nest to live on their own when they have moulted twice.

Earwigs may hide in tunnels, but rarely inside our ears! They are nocturnal and prefer to be outside, feeding on plants or any small insects they can find.

3-second sum-up

Most insects don't care for their young. Social insects and some solitary insects, such as earwigs, do.

3-minute mission Where are the ears?

Next time you see an earwig, take a close look at it with a magnifying glass – or just look at the earwig pictures on the opposite page. Can you find the earwig's 'ears'? Earwigs probably got their name because their wings, which lie folded up on their backs, look a bit like a pair of ears.

A female earwig finds a mate, makes a nest, lays her eggs, keeps them safe, and protects and feeds her nymphs after they hatch.

Male and female earwigs meet up in the autumn to mate.

The earwigs dig their nest burrow in the soil.

The eggs are tiny, white ovals.

The mother earwig turns the eggs over and keeps them clean.

When the eggs are ready to hatch, the female spreads them out to give them more space.

The nymphs look like tiny adults.

They go through four different stages as they grow, moulting each time.

After the second moult, young earwigs go off to live alone.

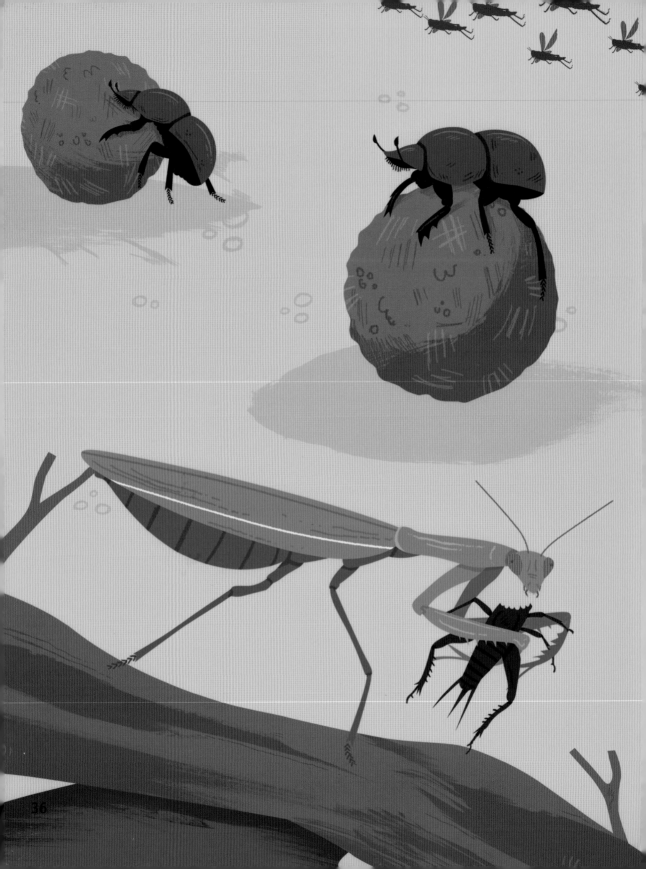

Insect food

Insects can spread out to live in all kinds of different places, and they can feed on many types of food, including plant leaves, fruits or flowers, other insects and small animals, and human leftovers. They also feed on animals much bigger than themselves, sucking their blood, nibbling on their bodies after they've died or even eating their poo! Some insects, like the dung beetle, prefer to stick to one type of food, while others, like cockroaches, will eat pretty much anything they can find.

Insect food
Glossary

aphids A group of insects that feed on plant sap and produce honeydew. They are one of the most damaging insect pests.

bacteria The simplest forms of life. They exist in large numbers in air, water and soil, in living and dead creatures, and in plants. They are often a cause of disease.

camouflage Markings or colours that allow an insect to blend in with its surroundings.

carcass The dead body or remains of an animal.

crops Plants that are grown in large quantities by farmers for food, such as maize and potatoes.

fungus (plural fungi) A living thing that isn't a plant or an animal, that feeds on organic matter, such as decaying leaves. Mushrooms and mould are both fungi.

honeydew The sweet substance excreted (pooed) by aphids.

nectar Sweet fluid released by flowers to attract insects and encourage pollination. Honeybees collect nectar to make honey.

pollen The yellow powder from the male part of a flower.

pollination The transfer of pollen from the male part of a flower to the female part, so that the flower can make seeds and reproduce.

prey The victim of a predator, usually killed for food.

regurgitate Bring swallowed food back up from the stomach into the mouth.

sap The fluid that flows inside a tree or plant.

scale insects Tiny plant-sucking insects covered by a protective scale. They latch on to a single plant and can cause serious damage.

scavenger An insect, for example a cockroach, that feeds on dead or decaying plants and animals, or leftover food.

spores Tiny, single-celled organisms released by a fungus, that develop into new adult fungi.

swarm A large group of flying or moving insects, such as locusts or bees.

symbiosis (sim-bi-osis) A close relationship between two different kinds of living things that depend on, and benefit from, one another.

Plant-eaters

... in 30 seconds

Insects can munch a lot of plants! Not all are plant-eaters, but those that are will often attack plants in such huge numbers that they can strip them bare.

A swarm of locusts can contain billions of hungry insects. They descend in a dark cloud and eat every scrap of a field of crops, such as maize. Termites feed on wood, especially dead wood. That could mean a fallen tree, or the timbers in a house. Sometimes a house can collapse, thanks to termites!

Tiny aphids pierce plant leaves or stems with their straw-like mouths to suck out the sugary sap, damaging or destroying many types of plants. Butterflies and moths lay their eggs on their favourite food plant. When they hatch, an army of caterpillars eats every leaf they can find to help them grow bigger and fatter.

Some plants, though, want insects to feed on them. They make nectar inside their flowers to attract bees and butterflies. The insects feed on the nectar without harming the flower. At the same time, they spread the plant's pollen from one flower to another. This helps the plant to make its seeds.

3-second sum-up

Some plant-eating insects eat huge numbers of plants, but some are helpful.

The ant tree

In central America, acacia ants live inside the large hollow thorns of the bull-horn acacia tree. They help the tree by stinging and fighting off animals that try to feed on it, and keeping the ground around it clear of other plants. In return, the tree makes nectar at the base of its leaves, and small, seed-like bundles of ant food that sprout from its leaf tips. Two species living together and helping each other like this is called symbiosis.

A swarm of hungry locusts descends on a maize crop – before long, there will be nothing left of it.

Desert locusts spend part of their lives alone, but after rain, they join together in big swarms.

A large swarm can eat enough food each day to feed a whole human city!

Locusts have sharp, slicing jaws, which are a bit like scissors, for biting and chewing food.

Each locust can eat roughly its own body weight – about 2 grams (0.7 oz) – of food in a day.

41

Fierce hunters

... in 30 seconds

Insects are small – even the biggest weigh no more than a banana! Yet in their own world, hunting insects can be as fierce and deadly as crocodiles, tigers and sharks are to humans.

Dragonflies and robber flies zoom through the air to chase down and catch their prey. They can outfly bees, butterflies, mosquitoes and most other insects. Other hunting insects hide, then snatch their victims as they pass by. The praying mantis sits still, looking like part of a plant, then suddenly grabs its prey with its front legs. An antlion larva digs a hollow in the sand, waits inside for ants to fall in, then grabs them with its sharp jaws.

Instead of biting jaws, the assassin bug has a sharp, pointed mouth like a needle. It uses this to stab through other insects' tough exoskeletons and inject a chemical that dissolves their insides – then it sucks the liquidized food back up.

The tarantula hawk wasp is even scarier. The female stings a much bigger tarantula, paralysing it. Then she drags it to her nest and lays an egg on it. When it hatches, the wasp larva burrows into the spider and eats it alive!

3-second sum-up

Savage hunting insects catch, grab, bite, sting or stab their prey.

3-minute mission Spot an insect alligator

Ladybird larvae are fearsome hunters that prowl plant stalks and leaves, gobbling up aphids, their favourite food. They are sometimes known as 'insect alligators'. They are about 1 cm (0.5 in) long, spiky and sausage-shaped. They have black, orange, yellow or green markings. You can spot them in the summer. To find them, carefully lift up plant leaves using a stick and take a look underneath. Don't touch – they can bite!

All around you, insects are busy hunting and catching their food – often other insects!

An assassin bug stabs its prey, an unlucky caterpillar.

This little fly is about to be grabbed by a big, fast dragonfly.

A praying mantis munches on a cricket while clasping it in its front legs.

A female tarantula hawk wasp attacks a huge tarantula by stinging its soft underside.

The wasp will drag the paralysed spider into her nest and lay an egg on it. It will be a living food supply for her larva.

Scavengers

... in 30 seconds

Cockroaches, earwigs and many types of ants are scavengers. They feed on dead plants and animals, or other animals' leftover food.

A long time ago, people thought flies actually grew from dead bodies, because they were often seen emerging from the carcass of a dead animal. In fact, this happens because flies lay their eggs in or on animal corpses. When the eggs hatch, the larvae, or maggots, feed on the rotting flesh until they are ready to turn into adults.

If you leave out a compost bin full of banana skins and apple cores, the same thing happens. Tiny fruit flies lay their eggs in the rotting fruit. A few days later, the bin will be buzzing with newly hatched flies.

A group of beetles called burying beetles find a small dead animal, such as a mouse or bird, dig a hole underneath it and bury it. A male and female beetle live in the hole, lay their eggs on the dead body and use it as food for their larvae when they hatch out.

These insects' diets might seem pretty disgusting, but they actually do a very important job. They clear away and dispose of dead creatures, stopping them from piling up and spreading germs.

3-second sum-up

Scavenging insects feed on dead animals, rotting plants and leftover food.

Medical maggots

Doctors use maggots in hospitals! As maggots love to nibble rotting flesh, they can be used to clean up wounds and injuries where part of the body has died and started to rot, such as frostbite. Once the maggots have removed the dead parts, it's easier for the living parts to heal up. (Medical maggots are specially bred to be clean and safe, not collected from bins or dead animals!)

Burying beetles can sniff a rotting dead animal from hundreds of metres away.

Scavenger insects eat dead and decaying matter. This is the gruesome way burying beetles prepare a tasty food store for their babies.

Pairs of beetles, one male and one female, will fight other pairs over the carcass, until one couple wins.

If necessary, the winning pair roll and push the body to a good spot. They roll it into a ball shape and cover it with a sticky substance to make it less smelly and harder for other scavengers to find.

The beetles dig under the animal so that it sinks into the ground.

The female lays eggs on the carcass. When the larvae hatch, the parents feed them by chewing up the dead animal and regurgitating the mushed-up food.

Farming
... in 30 seconds

Apart from humans, only a few types of animals can farm. They include some fish, snails and crabs, and several insect species.

Leafcutter ants farm fungus in their nests and so do many termite species. Inside their tall termite towers are special fungus gardens where – on a pile of chewed wood and plants mixed with their own poo – they grow fungus to eat.

Ambrosia beetles also farm fungi. They bore tunnels into trees and carry tiny spores of a special tree fungus inside. The fungus grows on the wood inside the tunnels, and provides food for the beetles and their larvae.

Some ant species, such as yellow meadow and black garden ants, farm other insects. They keep 'herds' of plant-eating aphids, guarding and protecting them while they feed. The ants stroke the aphids with their antennae to make them release a sweet substance called honeydew, which the ants eat.

Another type of ant keeps scale insects in nests under tree bark, but instead of honeydew, scientists think the ants might be farming them as food.

3-second sum-up

Some types of insects farm plants or animals for food.

3-minute mission Track farmer ants

Spot ants farming aphids by looking closely at plants that aphids love to feed on, such as:

• Roses (watch out for thorns!) • Honeysuckle • Tulips
• Pea and bean plants • Dahlias • Nasturtiums

Look for green or black aphids all over the plant's stems or leaves, with larger ants guarding them. If you're lucky, you might see the ants trying to fight off an aphid hunter, such as a ladybird.

Insect farmers, like these ants, beetles and termites, get their food from the animals, plants or fungi they look after.

These black garden ants are herding green aphids on the underside of a leaf.

The ants herd and round up the aphids. They will even carry them to good spots for feeding.

This ant is 'milking' an aphid for its honeydew.

The ants release chemicals that make the aphids slow and calm.

The honeydew is basically aphid poo!

Ambrosia beetles tend the fungus they grow in tunnels inside a tree.

Termites farm fungus, growing it in special 'fungus gardens' deep inside their nest.

Poo-eaters!

... in 30 seconds

Almost anything can become food for one type of insect or another – even poo! Poo-eating insects include cockroaches, flies and some types of ants and butterflies. They get the food they need from the bacteria in the poo, or from food that hasn't been fully digested by the animal that ate it.

Dung beetles are the champion poo-eaters among insects. There are thousands of species, and they live all over the world, mainly eating the poo of large mammals such as cows, buffaloes and elephants.

The beetles search for poo using their excellent sense of smell. Some species just lay their eggs in the dung, but others shape it into a ball, dig a burrow, then roll the dung ball into it. They can then use the dung as a food store, or lay eggs in it for the larvae to eat when they hatch.

Termites even eat each other's poo! This is because, to digest the wood they eat, they need a special type of bacteria in their guts. They can only get this bacteria by eating the poo from another termite.

3-second sum-up

Many types of insects feed on poo – especially dung beetles!

3-minute mission Make a scarab

The ancient Egyptians believed dung beetles were sacred, and they often carved dung beetle models and pendants, known as 'scarabs'.

You need: Air-drying modelling clay • Plastic knife or pencil

1 Form a beetle shape with a flat base and a rounded top.

2 Carve wings and eyes in the top and your name in the base. Make a small hole through it if you want a pendant. Leave to dry.

The dung beetles have sniffed out a fresh pile of dung – delicious!

On a bright night, dung beetles come out in search of poo!

The dung beetles collect the dung into a ball, ready to roll it away.

This beetle has climbed on top of its ball to get a good view of the sky and its route.

Sometimes one dung beetle will fight another over the best bits of poo.

The beetle uses the sun, moon or stars to help it move in a straight line away from the dung heap and away from the other beetles.

The ball is safely hidden in the beetle's burrow, ready for an egg to be laid in it.

Camouflage

... in 30 seconds

Besides needing to eat, most insects have to avoid being eaten by something else. Insects are food for all kinds of other animals, including many other insects, spiders, lizards, birds, fish, frogs, shrews, chimps and anteaters.

One good way to hide from enemies is to be hard to spot. So lots of insects have colours, markings and shapes that blend in perfectly with their surroundings, or mimic a less tasty object, such as a dry leaf or stick. You could walk through a forest and never notice that many of the leaves, twigs and sticks were actually living insects – such as the leaf insect, stick insect, dead leaf butterfly or leaf katydid.

Thorn bugs have spikes on their backs to make them look like thorns on the plant they are feeding on. The giant swallowtail butterfly caterpillar is disguised to look just like a disgusting bird dropping! And some insects, like the sand grasshopper and the peppered moth, are speckled and coloured so that they exactly match their habitat – a sandy desert and a tree trunk.

Hunting insects can also use camouflage. The flower mantis sits on a flowering plant pretending to be a flower, until its prey comes close enough to catch.

3-second sum-up

Many insects use camouflage to hide from their enemies or their prey.

3-minute mission Design a camouflaged bug

You need: Coloured pens or pencils • Paper and scissors

Find a patterned or textured surface such as a wooden floorboard, a woolly sweater or a patterned carpet. Now draw and colour in a moth or beetle that would be good at hiding there. When it's finished, cut it out and see how well it blends in.

Camouflage can protect insects from their prey. Can you spot all eight insects that are hiding here?

Flower mantis   Dead leaf butterfly   Giant swallowtail caterpillar   Thorn bug

Peppered moth   Sand grasshopper   Leaf insect   Stick insect

Eating us!

... in 30 seconds

Plenty of insects out there have a favourite food that is not plants, fungi or other insects, but you! Or at least a bit of you – usually a mouthful of your blood.

Mosquitoes are famous for their bloodsucking habits, but they mainly eat plant nectar and sap. Only female mosquitoes need blood when they are ready to lay their eggs. First, the mosquito zooms in on the smell of your breath and sweat. Then she pierces your skin with her needle-shaped mouth and sucks out enough blood to fill her up.

Midges, blackflies and horseflies can also suck your blood, often leaving a sore, painful or itchy spot. But they only visit us when they're hungry! Head lice actually live on us, hiding among our hair and holding on tight with their claws. Several times a day, they bite into the scalp to suck some blood.

Even worse, there are some insects – like botflies and tumbu flies – that can get under our skin. The fly larva tunnels inside and feeds on your flesh as it grows. Luckily, it then drops out to spend the rest of its life elsewhere!

3-second sum-up

Several types of flies and lice can feed on human blood, or live on or inside our bodies.

3-minute mission Eating them!

Insects can be a favourite food for humans, too! Match these wriggly snacks with the countries where they are popular:

- Midge burgers
- Mopane worms (a type of moth caterpillar)
- Escamoles (ant larvae)
- Inago (fried grasshoppers)
- Bogong moths

- Japan
- Australia
- Botswana
- Uganda
- Mexico

Answers on page 96

Watch out . . . hungry insects like these could be sizing you up for a snack!

Head lice love to live among a nice thick head of hair. They use their sharp mouths to bite your scalp and suck up your blood!

You might not feel it when a midge bites, but later your skin is horribly itchy!

The larva of a botfly like this could actually live under your skin!

Mosquitoes like to zoom in on your skin to suck up a bellyful of blood.

54

Insect homes

When you see a bee, wasp, beetle or butterfly buzzing or flapping around, do you wonder if it has a home to go to? Not all insects do – some just wander to and fro, find food and rest when they're tired. But many insects are skilful builders, burrowing homes under the ground or inside trees, or using wood, wax, mud or leaves to construct nests that can be amazingly big, clever and complicated. And a few insects make life easy for themselves by simply moving in with us.

Insect homes
Glossary

antenna (plural antennae) One of two sensitive feelers on top of an insect's head.

boring insect An adult insect or larva which make holes or tunnels into trees and plants.

chambers The 'rooms' in a large insect nest that are connected by tunnels, such as a food store, the larvae nursery, and the queen's quarters.

fungus (plural fungi) A living thing that isn't a plant or an animal, that feeds on organic matter, such as decaying leaves. Mushrooms and mould are both fungi.

gall A bumpy growth on a plant, such as a tree, made when an insect or insect larva injects chemicals into the plant. The insect uses the gall as a nest and a source of food.

gills Openings in the body of an underwater insect nymph or larva that take in oxygen from the water.

honeycomb The name for the hexagon-shaped (six-sided) cells of a honeybee's nest. The cells are made from wax that comes from the bees' bodies.

larva (plural larvae) A worm-like baby insect that looks different from its parents.

leaf miner The larva of a small fly, a beetle or a moth that burrows in between the two surfaces of a leaf.

mould A type of fungus.

ovipositor A hollow, tube-like organ that lets a female insect lay her eggs in an exact place.

surface tension The force in the surface layer of water that lets water insects move across it without sinking.

ventilate Let fresh air flow in and stale air flow out.

Plant-dwellers

... in 30 seconds

Any park, garden or forest is full of insects – the plants provide them with food, and make good hiding places. Some insects even make their homes inside plants.

Insects like acorn weevils and fig wasps lay their eggs inside a fruit, nut or flower bud that is just starting to grow. This gives the larva a supply of food and protects it from the weather and predators. Leaf miners are tiny moth caterpillars, or other insect larvae, that live inside leaves.

Some insects can actually drill or dig their way through tree bark and into the solid wood. Wood-boring beetles, such as the emerald ash borer, lay their eggs in cracks or hollows in tree bark. When the larvae hatch they nibble their way through to feed on the inner bark.

Female horntail wasps have an 'ovipositor' – an egg-laying tail spike. They drill it into a tree, then lay an egg under the bark. When the egg hatches the larva munches a tunnel through the wood. The ichneumon (ik-new-mon) wasp checks for the tiny movements made by wood wasp larvae. Then she uses her own ovipositor to drill through the bark and lays her own egg in the wood wasp larva! It feeds on the larva as it grows.

3-second sum-up

Some insects live inside plants, especially when they are larvae.

Insect power!

How can a tiny insect's tail bore into solid wood? An ovipositor has two sides that lock and push against each other, meaning the wasp does not have to push hard. In some species, the tip of the ovipositor releases a chemical that helps to dissolve the wood. And scientists have found that some ichneumon wasps have a lot of metal in their ovipositor tips, making them stronger.

A large tree, such as an ash, can have many kinds of insects living inside and on it.

This leaf has been damaged by a munching leaf miner.

Holes made by adult wood wasps when they emerged from inside the tree.

A horntail, or wood wasp, lays eggs under the bark.

A wood wasp larva inside its tunnel.

This giant ichneumon wasp is laying her egg in the wood wasp larva!

This fully-grown adult emerald ash borer has just crawled out of the tree.

An emerald ash borer larva is nibbling through the bark.

Underground living

... in 30 seconds

There are countless insects under your feet. Under the soil, sand or mud, insects dig out nests, tunnel for food or bury their eggs so that their larvae can grow there.

Ants and termites are famous for their large underground nests. Formosan termites can dig a network of tunnels and rooms stretching as far as 100 m (330 feet), to reach a good source of wood. When scientists excavated an old leafcutter ant nest in Brazil, it was the size of a human house!

Mole crickets get their name because they dig underground passageways, like moles do. These chunky insects have big, strong front legs for digging and huge heads for pushing through the soil. As they tunnel along, they feed on plant roots or other insects.

Wichetty grubs, the larvae of a type of moth, live in burrows among the roots of bushes in Australian deserts. They feed on the roots for up to two years and can grow to 10 cm (4 inches) long.

The deepest dwelling insects of all are those that live in caves, such as cave beetles and cave crickets. They often have poor eyesight or no eyes at all, as there is so little light to see by. Instead, they have extra-long, sensitive antennae to feel their way around.

3-second sum-up

Many types of insects live underground or in caves.

3-minute mission **A bee hotel**

Some bees, such as bumblebees and miner bees, make their nests in the soil, in a hole in a wall or under buildings. If you have a garden, you can give the bees more places to nest by leaving out old flower pots in quiet, undisturbed corners. Leave some flower pots upside down and others the right way up with some soil inside.

Mole crickets live in a system of underground tunnels.

What lies beneath the ground? It's not all solid earth – there are all kinds of insect homes there.

Inside a tall termite tower a vast network of tunnels and chambers stretches far underground.

Female mole crickets lay their eggs in a special nursery chamber.

There's not much to eat in a cave, but cave crickets feed on other small creepy-crawlies, or on mould.

In and below a termite tower live colonies of millions of tiny, sometimes blind, termites.

Home-building

... in 30 seconds

Like us, many insects use the materials they find around them to build their homes. Unlike us, some of them produce the building materials from their own bodies!

Mound-building termites construct tall towers from a mixture of mud, poo and saliva. Common wasps make paper by scraping bits off a wooden surface with their jaws and mixing it with saliva. They spit out the paper pulp and use it to build a nest made of hexagonal cells.

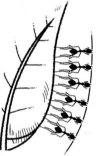

Weaver ants join leaves together to make their nests. They seal the leaf edges using sticky silk made by their larvae. Honeybees make their hexagon-shape honeycombs from wax that is released in tiny flakes from the undersides of their bodies. Insects that live alone can build, too. A female potter wasp shapes mud into a nest that looks like a tiny pottery jar.

One group of insects even has a way of tricking plants into making a home for them. Gall wasps and other gall insects release chemicals that make plants form bumps and growths. The insect can then make its home inside the lumpy gall, or use it as a safe place to lay its eggs.

3-second sum-up

Insects are skilful builders, making nests from many materials, some from their own bodies.

3-minute mission Gall-spotting

Look out for insect galls on the trees in your nearest park or on your trip to school. You might see:

Leaf galls: round, pointed or fluffy-looking small lumps that form on the surface of leaves.
Twig galls: round, bulging lumps growing either on the side of a twig, or surrounding it.

All of these amazing structures are built by insects, using the natural materials around them.

Gall wasps make lumpy galls grow on leaves for their larvae to grow inside.

Wasps' round, delicate nests are built from paper made from chewed wood.

Weaver ants glue leaves together to form a cosy chamber to live inside.

A solitary potter wasp shapes mud into a perfectly formed little pot as a nest for her young.

Water insects

... in 30 seconds

Ponds, lakes, streams and rivers are home to many kinds of water insects. Spotting such small creatures is sometimes tricky and you might have to look closely.

Pond skaters and whirligig beetles zip around on the water surface, using the surface tension to hold them up. They hunt flying insects that accidentally get trapped in the water, or dead ones that fall onto it.

Backswimmers, or water boatmen, swim using their long back legs like oars. Diving beetles dive deep underwater, carrying a bubble of air with them so that they can breathe. They hunt tadpoles and even small fish.

Dragonflies, stoneflies and caddis flies live deep underwater as larvae. They take oxygen from the water using their gills, or by soaking it up through their skin. Once they are big enough, they crawl out of the water to become flying adults.

Other water animals, like trout, salmon and frogs, love to eat water insects. Some insects zoom away fast to escape from danger, while others have fierce jaws to fight off enemies.

3-second sum-up

Many insects live on or under the water, especially insect young.

3-minute mission Surface tension test

You need: Bowl of water • Needles or paperclips • Kitchen paper

Put a needle or paperclip on a small piece of kitchen paper and lower it gently onto the water. It should rest on the surface. If you disturb the water, the needle or paperclip will sink.

Hardly any insects live in the sea.
Most water insects are found in
fresh water, like this pond.

Adult dragonflies fly
fast over the water,
chasing their prey.

Pond skaters detect the
ripples from prey landing in
the water through their feet.

Backswimmers swim
upside down, often
near the surface.

Whirligig beetles get their
name because they zoom
around and around in circles.

This great diving beetle is
grabbing a tasty tadpole.

Caddis fly larvae build a protective
case around their bodies, made of
sand, pebbles, shells or twigs.

Dragonfly larvae are jet-
propelled! They can shoot
water out of their bottoms to
escape from danger quickly.

House guests

... in 30 seconds

Ever since humans have been living in houses, all kinds of insects have decided to share our warm, comfortable homes with us.

For a start, we keep stores of food in our cupboards, inviting insects like ants, cockroaches and flour beetles to help themselves. Houseflies land and slurp on any food that is left lying around, and like to lay their eggs in our rubbish bins.

Instead of eating our food, some insects prefer feeding on our possessions. Clothes moths lay their eggs in clothes or carpets made of natural fibres, such as wool and silk. When the moth larvae hatch out they eat the fabric, leaving an annoying hole. Our carpets and blankets can also be munched by plump and furry carpet beetle larvae. A paper louse will even nibble through old books.

Silverfish like to live somewhere damp, so you might spot one in the bathroom. They eat mould, dandruff, hair and dead skin. A human home may also contain fleas living on pet dogs or cats, and bedbugs. Bedbugs hide in bedclothes or bed frames, and sneak out in the dark to suck blood from whoever is sleeping there!

3-second sum-up

Insects find food, warmth and shelter in human homes.

3-minute mission Fly cam

Set up a fly cam and catch feeding flies in action!

You need: Camera phone • Leftover food • Shallow container

1 Put a leftover sandwich, banana or cake in the container.

2 Lean the phone against the side and check the food is in view.

3 Set the phone to video record and leave the room!

Your home probably doesn't have all these insects living in it, but you might spot a few if you know where to look.

Furry carpet beetle larvae munch blankets and carpet fibres.

A silverfish lurks under the sink, waiting for falling flakes of skin or dandruff.

The family cat is itchy because of bites from the fleas living in its fur.

Houseflies spread germs onto the food they eat, as they spit on it to soften it. They usually poo on it, too!

A coat hung up on a hook has clothes moth larvae hiding under the collar.

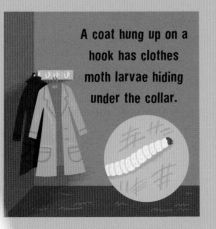

Cockroaches can live under kitchen cupboards. They come out at night to look for crumbs and dropped food.

Living together

Humans live in towns, cities and countries, sharing jobs and resources, and looking after each other when necessary. And there are some types of insects that do the same. Living together is a good way for each small, individual insect, such as an ant, to benefit from safety in numbers, a home and a steady food supply. In return, each member of the group has to do jobs that help the group as a whole, and defend it from danger.

Living together
Glossary

beeswax The substance that worker honeybees produce in tiny flakes from the underside of their bodies. The bees use it to build their honeycombs.

caste A group of insects in a colony that look and behave the same, and which do the same job, for example, workers and soldiers.

chambers The 'rooms' in a large insect nest that are connected by tunnels, such as a food store, the larvae nursery and the queen's quarters.

chimneys Open shafts or holes in a termite mound or ant nest that let air inside.

colony (plural colonies) A large group of insects from the same species, which live, work and communicate with one another.

comb A nest made up of hexagonal (six-sided) chambers, such as a wasps' nest.

drone A male bee without a sting. The drone's job is to mate with the queen.

fungus (plural fungi) A living thing that isn't a plant or an animal, that feeds on organic matter, such as decaying leaves. Mushrooms and mould are both fungi.

hibernate To sleep during the winter. Many adult insects shelter from the cold weather in trees, houses and leaf piles. They include bees, ladybirds and butterflies.

honey A food source for bees made from nectar collected by worker bees from plants. The bees make it by mixing the sweet nectar with chemicals from their bodies.

honeydew The sweet substance excreted (pooed) by aphids.

nectar Sweet fluid released by flowers to attract insects and encourage pollination. Bees collect nectar to make honey.

queen In a colony, the queen is usually the largest insect and the only one that can reproduce. She spends her life laying eggs and being cared for by the workers.

social insects Insects such as bees, wasps, ants and termites, which live together in a large group or colony.

soldiers In a colony, soldier insects are bigger than workers, with large heads and strong jaws for fighting. They protect the nest, the queen and the workers.

solitary insects Insects that live alone instead of in groups.

species The scientific name for a type of living thing that can reproduce to make more of the same type, for example, honeybees.

waggle dance A figure-of-eight dance performed by a worker honeybee to tell the colony where to find food or water.

workers In a bee colony, the female workers care for the queen and larvae, construct and clean the nest, and forage (search) for food.

ventilate Let fresh air flow in and stale air flow out of a structure, for example, an underground nest.

Social insects

... in 30 seconds

Insects that live together in big family groups, or colonies, are called social insects. They include ants, termites and some species of bees and wasps. Social insects are very widespread and numerous. In fact, there are far more of them on our planet than there are of other types of insect. In some species, there can be millions of insects living in just one colony.

The insects in a colony don't just live together, they work together. For example, they will co-operate to do jobs that one insect couldn't do on its own, such as building a large nest. They also share the work, taking turns to do tasks like finding food and looking after larvae.

Most colonies have a queen. She is often larger than the others and spends her life laying eggs. The members of a colony devote their lives to protecting their colony and queen. Individual ants or bees may die fighting off a threat, so that the colony can survive.

Some scientists have described insect colonies as being like a single creature, made up of many individual parts. The parts can move around on their own but think and behave as one. Because of this, an insect colony is sometimes called a 'superorganism'.

3-second sum-up

Social insects live in large groups or colonies. They all work together to help the colony survive.

3-minute mission Work together

See what it's like to be part of a colony. Grab some friends and work together on a task. It could be building a house out of Lego, or making a picture using coloured beads or buttons. But remember, just like insects, there's no talking!

How will you communicate with each other, make a plan and share out the jobs?

Working together, these ants can catch and drag home prey that is much bigger than they are.

These ants have surrounded an unlucky millipede.

Some of the ants grab and pull the millipede . . .

. . . while others go around to the other side to push.

More ants have formed long 'daisy chains', like humans would in a tug of war, to give them extra pulling force.

Together the ants will drag the heavy millipede back to their nest.

Ant colonies

... in 30 seconds

The biggest colonies of all are made by ants. A colony of driver or safari ants can contain over 20 million ants – similar to the number of humans in the world's biggest cities.

Like other social insects, the ants in a colony have their own roles. The colony is led by the queen, which lays eggs and controls the other ants using chemical signals. Some colonies have more than one queen.

Hundreds, thousands or millions of worker ants do all the jobs that keep the colony alive, like looking after eggs and babies, finding food and building the colony nest. In some colonies, fierce soldier ants fight off enemies with their large jaws. There are also some male ants with the job of mating with queens to start new colonies. Queens and males that are looking for a mate are the only ants that have wings.

Many types of ants dig their nests in the soil, with lots of tunnels and rooms. But some species make nests in sand, in dead logs, in tree branches or leaves, or inside plant roots. Driver ants can even cling together to make their own bodies into a temporary nest, with a safe space inside for the queen.

3-second sum-up

Ant colonies can be made up of many millions of ants living together.

Supercolonies!

Scientists have found that a type of ant, called the Argentine ant, makes a colony that can stretch across many nests. A 'supercolony' like this can have thousands of queens and hundreds of millions of workers. Ants from different colonies normally fight each other, but the ants in a supercolony all recognise each other by their colony smell, and are friendly.

Millions of ants live together in a huge underground nest, like these leafcutter ants, found in North and South America.

Tall chimneys and other holes ventilate the nest.

The ants collect pieces of leaves and carry them back to the nest.

The ants dig lots of chambers connected by tunnels.

The collected leaves are stored in special food chambers. A whitish fungus grows on them.

When the eggs hatch, the larvae feed on the fungus.

The Queen ant sits in the fungus to lay her eggs.

Waste leaves are taken to rubbish dump chambers.

Honeybee combs
... in 30 seconds

Not all species of bees are social insects – some are 'solitary' and live alone. Honeybees, however, live in large colonies and are the best-known social insects.

A typical colony has one queen, some drones (male bees) and up to 80,000 worker bees. The workers are all female, but do not lay eggs – only the queen does that. Workers do a series of jobs including cleaning the hive, feeding the larvae, building new honeycomb and flying out to collect food. The drones' job is to mate with other queen bees to start new colonies.

Bees make honey from nectar, a sweet liquid found in flowers. They mix it with chemicals inside their stomach, then regurgitate it into a cell where it dries out and becomes thicker and stickier. Bees use honey as stored food for themselves and their larvae.

Wild honeybees build nests out of beeswax from their bodies, in the form of honeycombs made up of hexagon-shaped cells. They store eggs and larvae in some cells, and honey in others. However, many honeybees build their combs inside hives provided by humans. We keep bees for their honey, and also because they spread pollen from flower to flower, helping us to grow food.

3-second sum-up

Honeybees live in wax nests or hives, and make honey as a way to store food.

3-minute mission Handy hexagons

Draw some hexagon-shaped cells and some round cells. Pack them tightly together on the page like a honeycomb. Which shapes fit together the best?

Bees and wasps both build hexagon-shaped cells because hexagonal cells fit tightly and can share walls. Hexagons make the greatest number of cells with the least amount of wax.

A honeycomb is always buzzing with bees,
some feeding larvae, some storing honey and
some communicating with each other.

These cells contain stored
honey and are covered
with a pale wax cap.

The Queen looks similar
to the worker bees, but
bigger. She releases
chemicals that the other
bees can smell, which helps
to control their behaviour.

Worker bees reach
into the cells to put
honey there, or to
feed the larvae.

Honey bees can 'talk' to each
other about where they have
found food, using a dance
called the waggle dance.

There are bee larvae
inside these cells.

The dance shows the
direction of the food
and how far away it is.

Wasps' nests

... in 30 seconds

Only a few species of wasps are social, but they are the most common. They are the yellow-and-black striped wasps that you see in the summer, buzzing around bins and bothering you when you have a picnic. They live in colonies of up to 12,000 and make paper nests.

A wasp colony starts when a young queen finds a good place for a nest. She scrapes wood from trees, buildings or fences with her jaws, mixes it with her saliva and shapes it into a 'comb' made up of six-sided chambers. Once there are a few chambers, she lays eggs in them and new wasps hatch.

These worker wasps then take over the job of building the nest, while the queen lays more eggs. A wasps' nest can grow up to a metre (3 ft) in one summer. The workers also fly out to find food. They prefer sweet, sugary food for themselves, but hunt animals such as moths, caterpillars and flies to feed the larvae. The larvae that get fed the most become new queens.

In the autumn, the first queen usually dies and the colony begins to break down. The wasps start to run out of food and may even eat each other. By winter they all die, except for the new young queens. After mating with a male, the queens hibernate somewhere sheltered until spring.

3-second sum-up

Social wasps are black and yellow, and build nests from paper made from wood.

3-minute mission Learn wasp first aid!

Wasps can be aggressive and sting lots of times. If you or someone you are with gets stung:

- Use ice wrapped in a cloth to cool down the area around the sting.

- Watch out for an allergic reaction. Call an ambulance if the person feels dizzy or faint, has a swollen face or tongue, gets a rash, or has trouble breathing.

This typical common wasps'
nest is built entirely of paper
made from chewed wood.

The Queen chooses somewhere safe
and sheltered to start the nest,
such as a tree, a hole in the ground
or an attic or cellar.

To make the paper,
the wasps scrape tiny
amounts of wood from
trees or wooden objects.

The workers chew
and mush up the wood
and use it to build the
nest's paper walls.

Like bees, the wasps
make a 'comb' of
hexagonal cells for
their larvae to grow in.

Worker wasps bring back
a supply of food for the
Queen and the larvae.

Termite towers

... in 30 seconds

On its own, a worker termite can't do much. It's a small, pale insect with a soft, squashy body, and it's also completely blind in some species. But working together as a colony, termites can stay safe, guard their queen, farm their own food and – in some species – build themselves huge, towering nests, known as termite mounds.

Tower-building termites are found in Africa, Australia, South America and Asia. One famous species, *Macrotermes bellicosus*, can construct mounds higher than a house. This takes a long time, but a colony can exist for ten years or more. At any one time, there can be over a million termites living there.

The workers build their tower by collecting clay and soil and mixing it with their own saliva and poo. Outside, the mound hardens in the sun, giving it strong walls to protect against predators. But inside, it stays warm and humid, and the mud and soil stay soft, so the termites can keep rebuilding and reshaping the rooms and tunnels.

For food, the termites collect dead plant material and bring it into the nest. Some of the termites eat the plants, while others feed on a type of fungus that they grow on a mixture of chewed plants and poo.

3-second sum-up

Termites can have colonies of a million or more, and some build tall mounds as nests.

Exploding termites!

Many other animals try to feed on termites, so they have a few clever ways of putting them off. Some can squirt their poo out at high speed. Scientists have also found a species in South America that can explode! Older workers build up a store of a toxic blue chemical on their backs. When the colony is in danger, they can burst to spray the enemy with poison.

A colony of *Macrotermes bellicosus* termites has several castes (different types) of termite living in it. Most of the termites are workers.

Workers

The workers can do different jobs: nest-building, caring for the Queen and nymphs, and going out foraging.

Queen

A Queen termite is one of the biggest, heaviest insects of all! She spends all her time laying eggs.

Soldiers

Soldiers are much bigger than workers. They have massive jaws for fighting enemies and guarding the workers.

Some types of termites also have a king. He is the Queen's mate and stays with her in her special chamber.

Insects and humans

People often get annoyed, upset or even scared if a fly lands on their lunch, or if a bee buzzes too close to them. We're used to insects helping themselves to our food, getting in our way and sometimes biting or stinging us. This can be a nuisance, and even dangerous – some serious diseases are spread by insects. However, insects are not just pests. While some can cause problems, others are useful. And there are some insects that we couldn't live without.

Glossary

allergic Having a bad reaction to something, such as the venom in an insect bite or sting, which can cause a rash, swelling or even make it hard to breathe.

boring insect An adult insect or larva which make holes or tunnels into trees and plants.

crops Plants, such as maize and potatoes, that are grown in large quantities by farmers for food.

helpful insect An insect that is useful and important to humans. For example, honeybees that pollinate our crops, and scavenger insects that clear away dead matter and stop germs from spreading.

pest insect A destructive insect that damages crops, plants, animals and people! Colorado potato beetles, gypsy moths, tsetse (say 'set-see') flies, cockroaches and head lice are all examples of insect pests.

pollination The transfer of the pollen from the male part of a flower to the female part, so that the flower can make seeds and reproduce.

species The scientific name for a particular type of living thing, which can reproduce to make more of the same type for example, honeybees.

spores Tiny, single-celled organisms released by a fungus, that develop into new adult fungi.

swarm A large group of flying or moving insects, such as locusts or bees.

venom The poisonous substance produced by some insects, such as bees and wasps, that is transferred by a sting or bite.

Insect pests

... in 30 seconds

We share our world with insects, and there are many, many more of them than there are of us. For each human, there are over 100 million insects! They all need food and places to live. And that means that some species of insects cause us all kinds of problems.

When farmers grow crops, they provide insects with whole fields of fresh, juicy food to feast on. Each crop has its own creepy-crawlies that love to eat it. Colorado potato beetles can munch through whole crops of potatoes or tomatoes. Coffee-borers burrow inside the fruits of coffee plants to lay their eggs. Boll weevils eat the flower buds of cotton plants, so they cannot form their fluffy 'bolls' of cotton.

In Africa, tsetse flies spread diseases in cows, horses and pigs that weaken or kill millions of animals. Gypsy moths and bark beetles can kill whole forests of trees.

In our homes, houseflies, wasps or cockroaches grab any food they can. Meanwhile, termites or carpenter ants munch through the wooden frames of houses; fleas, bedbugs and head lice make us itch; and midges bite us when we go camping or hiking!

3-second sum-up

Many types of insects are pests that cause problems for humans.

3-minute mission Don't get eaten!

These tips should help you to avoid becoming a feast for midges or 'no-see-ums' next time you're camping or in the outdoors:

- Midges are attracted to dark colours, so wear light ones.
- Eat garlic – midges hate the smell of it.
- Stay in the sunshine if possible – midges prefer shade.
- If midges attack, fan yourself – they don't like wind.
- Skin cream, sun cream or body lotion will help to stop midges biting you.

In many crop fields there is a constant battle between farmers and crop-munching insects.

The potato crop will soon be ready to harvest – but it's being eaten by Colorado beetles and their larvae.

The farmer sprays spores of a special fungus that attacks the beetles.

The red, spotted larvae feed on the leaves, badly damaging the crop.

The stripy yellow adult beetles munch on the leaves and lay lots of eggs.

This predator, a type of ground beetle, can control Colorado beetles by eating their eggs and larvae.

Dangerous insects

... in 30 seconds

Can a small creepy-crawly really be a deadly killer?
The answer is yes – several types of insects can kill humans.
These are the ones to look out for!

One of the scariest insects of all is the Asian giant hornet, found mainly in Japan. It's a huge wasp, up to 5 cm (2 in) long, with a sting so painful that it is said to feel like having a burning hot nail stuck into you! And if several hornets sting at once (which they often do), the venom can be lethal.

Normal-sized wasps and honeybees can be dangerous too, especially for anyone allergic to their stings, or if they sting in a swarm. Killer bees are unusually aggressive honeybees that sometimes attack people.

South America's giant silkworm moth can't hurt you, but its caterpillar can. It is covered in needle-like hairs that break off and stick into anyone who touches it. They inject a venom so powerful that people often die from it.

The deadliest insects of all spread diseases when they bite and suck our blood. In the past, fleas killed millions by spreading the killer disease bubonic plague. Mosquitoes still harm thousands of people by spreading diseases such as malaria and yellow fever.

3-second sum-up

A few species of insects can be extremely dangerous to humans.

3-minute mission Imagine an insect

Scientists are discovering hundreds of new species of insects every year. Draw and colour a picture of the bug you would like to find. How big is your insect? What defences does it use? Is it deadly or helpful to humans? Can it fly? What does it eat and who or what are its enemies? Name your insect.

These are some of the world's deadliest insects. How would you rank them in order of most to least dangerous?

50 mm
(2 inches)

The Asian giant hornet is one of the world's biggest wasps, and has one of the most painful of all insect stings.

The honeybee is normally a peaceful insect – but in killer bee form, it can attack in a deadly swarm.

18 mm
(0.7 inch)

3.3 mm
(0.1 inch)

Fleas have a pretty harmless bite – unless they happen to be carrying deadly germs.

16 mm
(0.6 inch)

55 mm
(2.2 inches)

The giant silkworm moth caterpillar has deadly stinging hairs that contain the most dangerous venom in the insect world.

Like fleas, malaria mosquitoes aren't dangerous themselves, but the germs they spread cause deadly diseases such as malaria.

Helpful insects

... in 30 seconds

While some insects can be a nuisance, there are others that are very useful. In fact, there are some insects that are so important to humans, it would be a disaster if we had to do without them!

The most useful insect of all has to be the honeybee. Besides providing honey and beeswax, bees pollinate many of our crops. We rely on them to carry pollen between flowers so that crops like apples and pears, raspberries, pumpkins, coffee and sunflowers can produce their fruits and seeds.

Several insects produce useful substances that humans collect. Shellac, used to make varnish, furniture polish, paints, dyes and food glazes, comes from the lac bug. The bugs make the smooth, shiny shellac as a covering for their eggs. For thousands of years, humans have been farming silk moths to harvest the fine threads that their caterpillars spin around themselves when they change into a pupa. The threads are spun and woven together to make silk fabric.

Insects are also great at cleaning up. Scavenging ants, dung beetles, burying beetles, earwigs and other insects feed on animal poo, dead animals and plants. They clear them away, keeping the ground clean and helping to recycle them back into the soil. Museums even use some types of beetles to clean the flesh off old animal skeletons, so they are ready to display.

3-second sum-up

Insects such as silk moths, lac bugs and honeybees are very useful to humans.

3-minute mission Be a helpful human

Honeybee numbers are growing smaller but you can help them to survive: plant flowers that make nectar and pollen (food for bees!); support beekeepers by buying local honey; and if a honeybee flies too close, don't swat it! Stay still and calm until it flies off.

The almond trees are in flower and ready to be pollinated so that the nuts can grow.

Honeybees are our most helpful insect. We use them to pollinate crops that will make the fruit and seeds we collect for food.

A stack of hives has been delivered to this almond orchard.

The beekeeper releases the honeybees.

The bees come out of the hives and head for the nearest food – the almond flowers!

The bees pick up pollen on their bodies as they visit the flowers, and it brushes off onto other flowers, pollinating them.

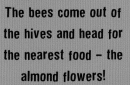

Discover more

BOOKS

Beetles (Really Weird Animals)
by Clare Hibbert
Franklin Watts, 2015

Butterflies and Moths (Really Weird
Animals) by Clare Hibbert
Franklin Watts, 2015

Insect by Laurence Mound
DK Eyewitness Books, 2008

Insects (Pocket Eyewitness)
DK, 2012

Insects (Naturetrail) by Rachel Firth
and Louie Stowell
Usborne, 2014

Inside a Beehive (The Magic School
Bus) by Joanna Cole
Scholastic, 1996

Minibeasts, Spiders and Insects
(Deadly Factbook) by Steve Backshall
Orion, 2014

The Book of Beetles by Patrice
Bouchard and Yves Bousquet
Ivy Press, 2014

*The Ultimate Bugopedia: The Most
Complete Bug Reference Ever* by
Darlyne Murawski and Nancy Honovich
National Geographic Kids, 2013

Ugly Bugs (Horrible Science)
by Nick Arnold
Scholastic, 2008

DVDS

Ants: Backyard Science
Phoenix Learning Group, Inc., 2013

Butterfly and Moth
Eyewitness Videos, 2006

Life in the Undergrowth
David Attenborough
BBC, 2005

The Fascinating World of Insects
BrainFood Learning, 2011

WEBSITES

antARK
http://antark.net

theBigBuzz
http://www.thebigbuzz.biz

Bug Facts
http://www.bugfacts.net

Buglife
https://www.buglife.org.uk

The Bee Cause
http://www.foe.co.uk/page/the-bee-cause-about

Insects.org
http://www.insects.org

National Geographic Kids
http://www.ngkids.co.uk

Natural History Museum
http://www.nhm.ac.uk/discover.html

The Amateur Entomologist's Society
http://www.amentsoc.org/bug-club/

The Royal Entomological Society
http://www.royensoc.co.uk

BBC nature
http://www.bbc.co.uk/nature/life/Insect/by/rank/all

APPS

Insects and Bugs
Amazon Media, 2013

Insects and Spiders Guide
Amazing Apps, 2014

Although every endeavour has been made by the publisher to ensure that all content from these websites is educational material of the highest quality and is age appropriate, we strongly advise that Internet access is supervised by a responsible adult.

Index